MACHINE LEARNING

THE ULTIMATE BEGINNERS GUIDE TO UNDERSTANDING

MACHINE LEARNING BASICS & TECHNIQUES

Richard Dumont

Copyright Notice.

Table of Contents

CHAPTER ONE

What is learning

Learning, like intelligence, covers such a broad range of processes that it is difficult to define precisely. A dictionary definition includes phrases such as "to gain knowledge, or understanding of, or skill in, by study, instruction, or experience," and "modification of a behavioural tendency by experience." Zoologists and psychologists study learning in animals and humans. In this book, we focus on learning in machines.

Nowadays, machine learning is a popular word, generally in relation to artificial intelligence and big data. But have any idea what precisely it is? It is actually artificial intelligence's sub-set where computer algorithms are utilized for learning data and information autonomously. Machine learning computers have the ability to change and enhance their algorithms all by themselves.

It's completely about listing computers in the job of sorting via huge amount of data which modern technology has enabled us to produce (also known as Big Data). Its prime focus is on the growth of computer programs which can teach themselves for emerging and changing when unveiled to new data.

Types of Data They Deal With

Machine Learning algorithms are wide range of tools; online learning tools predict data on the fly. These tools are capable of learning trillions of observations one by one. They predict and learn simultaneously. Other algorithms like Random Forest and Gradient Boosting are also exceptionally fast with large data.

However, statistical modelling is generally applied for smaller data with fewer attributes or end up above the fit.

Predictive Power and Human Effort

The smaller assumptions in the predicted model will be the prognostic power. Machine learning, as the name implies, requires a minimal effort. Machine learning works on repetitions where the computer tries to find patterns hidden in the data. Since the machine works on comprehensive data and is independent of all assumptions, predictive power is usually very strong for these models.

The statistical model is intensive in mathematics and is based on coefficient estimation. This requires the model to understand the relationship between the variable before it is introduced.

There are several parallels between animal learning and machine learning. Indeed, many techniques in machine learning derive from the efforts of psychologists to make more accurate their theories of animal and human learning through computational models. It also seems likely that the concepts and techniques that researchers are exploring in machine learning can illuminate certain aspects of biological learning.

It is very interesting to know the applications of machine learning. Google and Facebook use Machine learning extensively to push their respective ads to the relevant users. Here are a few applications that you should know:

- Banking & Financial services: Machine learning can be used to predict the customers who are likely to default from paying loans or credit card bills. This is of paramount importance as machine learning would help the banks to identify the customers who can be granted loans and credit cards.

- Healthcare: It is used to diagnose deadly diseases (e.g. cancer) based on the symptoms of patients and tallying them with the past data of similar kind of patients.
- Retail: It is used to identify products which sell more frequently (fast moving) and the slow moving products which help the retailers to decide what kind of products to introduce or remove from the shelf.

Also, machine learning algorithms can be used to find which two / three or more products sell together. This is done to design customer loyalty initiatives which in turn help the retailers to develop and maintain loyal customers.

Essentiality of Machine Learning:

Presently, computers are enabled by machine learning algorithms to interact with humans, find terrorist suspects, write and publish sport match reports and drive cars autonomously. This will influence many industries and the jobs within them, and for this purpose, every manager must have some grasp at least of what machine learning is and how it is developing.

Currently, it is possible for machine to quickly create models which can analyse more complex and bigger data and supply more relevant and faster results, in fact on a larger scale. And by producing exact models, a company has a better opportunity to identify profitable chances or ignoring strange risks.

How IoT can advantage from Machine Learning:

IoT machines are producing a massive amount of data and machine learning is completely being employed for analyzing and reading that data in order to help enhance client service and efficiency, and lessen energy consumption and costs. For producing a good learning system, you require:

- Ensemble modeling
- Scalability
- Iterative and automation process
- Basic and advanced algorithms
- Data preparation capabilities

Air quality and energy with Machine Learning:

Air quality and several types of energy consumption implement artificial intelligence, cloud computing and big data for mapping nonlinear and complex air pollution trends effectively and relevantly. The technique employs deep machine learning and provides intelligent tips to managers and users on saving energy and getting better air quality. Now the solutions can be suggested by machine learning, thanks to this technology. In fact, the equipment can be identified from a single metering point.

For getting the most value from machine learning, you should know about pairing the best algorithms with the correct processes and tools. Although, this is one of the largest trends to detect everything and anything nowadays, more research needs to be done for testing the algorithm

Wellsprings of Machine Learning

Work on machine learning is now converging from several sources. These different traditions bring different methods and different vocabularies that are now being assimilated into a more unified discipline. Here is a brief list of some of the separate disciplines that have contributed to machine learning;

- **Brain models**: non-linear elements with weighted inputs as simple models of biological neurons. The networks of these elements have been studied by several researchers, including [McCulloch and Pitts, 1943, Hebb, 1949, Rosenblatt, 1958] and, more recently, by Gluck and Rumelhart, 1989, Sejnowski, Koch and Churchland, 1988. Brain models are interested in the proximity of these networks to the learning phenomena of Living brains. Several important machine learning techniques are based on networks of nonlinear elements - often called neural networks. Work inspired by this school is sometimes called connectionism, brain-style computing, or sub-symbolic processing.

- **Statistics**: A long-standing problem in statistics is the best way to use samples taken from unknown probability distributions to help decide which distribution a new sample is drawn from. A related problem is how to estimate the value of an unknown function at a new point given the values of this function in a set of sampling points. Statistical methods for dealing with these problems can be considered as machine learning cases because decision and estimation rules depend on a corpus of samples drawn from the problematic environment.

- **Theory of adaptive control**: Control theorists study the problem of controlling a process that has unknown parameters that must be estimated during operation. Often, the parameters change during operation, and the control process must track these changes. Some aspects of controlling a robot based on sensory inputs represent examples of this type of problem.

- **Psychological Models**: Psychologists have studied the performance of humans in various learning tasks. An early example is the EPAM network for storing and retrieving one member of a pair of words when given another. Related work led to a number of the early decision tree and semantic network methods. More recent work of this sort has been influenced by activities in artificial intelligence which we will be presenting. Some of the work in reinforcement learning can be traced to efforts to model how reward stimuli influence the learning of goal-seeking behavior in animals [Sutton & Barto, 1987]. Reinforcement learning is an important theme in machine learning research.

- **Psychological models**: Psychologists have studied the performance of people in different learning tasks. The first example is EPAM network storage and retrieval of one member of a pair of words when given different [Figenbaum, 1961]. The work related to many ways to make an early decision [Hunt, Marin, Stone, 1966] and the Network of Marks [Anderson and Bauer, 1973]. Recent studies of this type of activity have been affected in the field of artificial intelligence, and we are now. Some work to promote learning can be attributed to the modeling efforts how reward incentives affect the learning of targeted research behavior in animals [Sutton and Barto, 1987]. Promoting learning is an important subject of learning machine research.

- **Artificial intelligence**: From the beginning, the research dealt with the learning machine AI. Samuel developed a prominent early program which identified the function parameters to evaluate positions on board in the ladies' game [Samuel, 1959]. AI researchers also examined the role of measurement in education (Carbonell, 1983), and how actions and decisions can be based on past ideal cases [Kolodner, 1993]. Recent work has focused on exploring the rules of expert systems using decision-making techniques [Quinlan, 1990] and on logic programming [Muggleton, 1991 Lavrač and Džeroski, 1994]. Another topic has been providing and disseminating the results of problem-solving through education based on the interpretation [DeJong

- **Evolutionary models**: Of course not only individual animals learn to work better, but species evolve so that they adapt to individual niches. Because the difference between development and learning can be evident in computer systems and techniques that have been proposed, some typical aspects of biological evolution has a means of learning to improve the performance of computer programs. Genetic algorithms [Netherlands, 1975] and genetic programming [Koza 1992, Koza, 1994], the most important computing techniques for development.

Relations to Other Fields

As a multidisciplinary field, learning machine exchange common themes with mathematical fields of statistics, information theory, game theory, and optimization. Is naturally a subfield of computer science, our goal is to program machines so that they learn. In some sense, automatic learning can be seen as a branch of artificial intelligence, where, after all, the ability to transform expertise into experience or to detect meaningful patterns in complex sensory data is the cornerstone of human and animal intelligence.

However, one should note that, in contrast to conventional AI, automated learning does not attempt to build an automated imitation of intelligent behavior, but rather to use the strengths and special abilities of computers to complement human intelligence, often performing tasks that fall outside human abilities. For example, the ability to scan and manipulate huge databases allows automated learning programs to detect patterns that are beyond the scope of human cognition. An element of experience, or training, in automated learning often refers to data that is generated randomly. The task of the learner is to address such randomly generated examples to draw conclusions about the environment in which these examples are selected.

This description of machine learning highlights its close relationship with statistics. In fact, there are many commonalities between the two disciplines, in terms of both objectives and techniques used. However, there are some important differences in focus; if the doctor comes to the hypothesis of a relationship between smoking and heart disease, the role of a statistic in the presentation of patients' samples and validation of this hypothesis (this is the common statistical task to test the hypothesis). In contrast, automated learning aims to use data collected from patient samples to arrive at a description of the causes of heart disease.

The hope is that automated techniques may be able to know meaningful patterns (or hypotheses) that may have been missed by the human observer. In contrast to traditional statistics, in general, learning automation, in this book in particular, algorithm considerations play a major role. Machine learning is about the implementation of learning by computers. Thus the algorithm issues are pivotal. We develop algorithms for learning tasks and we are concerned about their computational efficiency.

The other difference is that while statistics are often interested in asymmetric behavior (such as the convergence of statistical estimates based on a sample as sample sizes grow to infinity), the focus of automated learning theory is on limited sample boundaries. Specifically, given the size of the samples available, the automatic learning theory aims to determine the degree of precision that a learner can expect based on these samples.

There are other differences between these two disciplines, which will mention just one more here. While it is common in statistics to operate under the assumption of some previously published data models (such as the assumption of normal data generation distributions, or the linear dependence of functional dependencies), in automated learning the emphasis is on working under "free distribution", where the learner assumes the least Possible about the nature of data distribution and allows the learning algorithm to see which models converge the best data generation process.

Few Useful Things to Know about Machine Learning

1. Learning = representation + evaluation + optimization

All automated learning algorithms have three components:

- Learner representation is a set if workbooks/functions that can be learned. This space group is called Hypothesis. If the function is not in the space hypothesis, it cannot be learned.
- Evaluation function tells how a good learning machine model is.
- Optimization is a way to search for an optimal learning model.

2. Circulation which is calculated

The primary goal of automated learning is to generalize out of the training package. The data used to evaluate the model should remain separate from the data used to learn the model. When we use circularization as a goal, we do not have access to a function that we can improve. Therefore, we must use training error as an alternative to the test error.

3. Data alone is not enough

Since our ultimate goal is generalization there is nothing like "adequate" data. There is a need to know beyond the data for generalization outside the data. Another way to develop is "no learner can overcome random guessing on all possible functions." But instead of coding assumptions, learners should allow the assumptions to be explicit, varied and automatically integrated into the form.

4. Overfitting has many faces

One way to explain overload is to divide the circular error into two components: bias and contrast. Bias is the tendency of the learner to constantly learn the same wrong thing (in the picture, the higher bias means more distance from the center). Contrast is the tendency to learn random things regardless of the signal (in the picture, high contrast means more scattered points).

A more powerful learner does not need to be better than the less powerful learner, where there can be considerable variation, while noise is not the only cause of overheating, it can actually exacerbate the problem. Against abuses are validations, organization, testing of statistical significance, etc.

5. Intuition failure in high dimensions

Properly circularization becomes doubly harder as dimensions (number of features) become large. Automated learning algorithms rely on a similarity-based thinking that collapses in high dimensions as the fixed-size training group covers only a small portion of the large input area. Moreover, our intuition of three-dimensional space often does not apply to the higher dimensional spaces. Even a dimensional curse may outweigh the benefits of having more features. However, in most cases, learners benefit from the grace of non-uniformity where data points are concentrated in multidimensional branches. Learners can benefit implicitly from this least effective dimension or use dimensional reduction techniques.

6. The theoretical guarantees are not what they considered

A common type of common correlation when dealing with automated learning algorithms relates to the number of samples needed to ensure good circulation. But these limits are very loose in nature. Moreover, the binding says that due to the sufficiently sufficient training data set, our learner will return a good hypothesis with a high probability or will not find a consistent hypothesis. They do not tell us anything about how to choose a good premise space.

Another common type of boundary is the oscillator binding which says "Given infinite data, the learner is guaranteed to produce the correct workbook." But in practice we never have data and infinite data alone is not enough. Therefore, theoretical safeguards should be used to understand and push the design of the algorithm rather than as a single criterion for determining the algorithm.

7. Engineering feature is the key

Machine learning is an iterative process where we train the learner, analyze the results, and modify the learner/data and replicate. Engineering feature is a crucial step in this pipeline. Having an appropriate type of features (independent features that are well associated with a class) makes learning easier. But the geometry of properties is also difficult because it requires domain-specific knowledge that goes beyond mere existing data.

8. More data beats intelligent algorithm

As a general rule, a dumb algorithm with lots of data beats a smart algorithm with a modest amount of data. But more data means more incremental issues. Learners of fixed size can use the data only to some extent after adding more data does not improve the results. Variable volume learners (non-parametric learners) can, in theory, learn any function due to an adequate amount of data. Of course, non-parametric learners are bound by the limits of memory and computational power.

9. Learn many models, not just one

In the early days of automated learning, the model or learner to be trained was predetermined and the focus was on tuning it to achieve optimal performance. Then the focus shifted to trying many variables of different learners.

When Do We Need Machine Learning?

When do we need to learn the machine instead of directly programming computers to carry out the task at hand? Two aspects of a particular problem may require the use of programs that learn and improve on the basis of their "experience": the complexity of the problem and the need for adaptation. Tasks those are very complex for the program.

- Functions performed by animals/humans: There are many tasks that we humans routinely perform, but our meditation on how to do them is not detailed enough to extract a well-defined program. Examples of such tasks are leadership, speech recognition, and understanding of images. In all these tasks, advanced learning programs and "learning from their experiences" programs have achieved quite satisfactory results once they have experienced enough training examples.
- Tasks beyond human capacity: A wide range of functions that utilize automated learning techniques are related to the analysis of large and very complex data sets:

astronomical data, conversion of medical archives into medical knowledge, weather forecasting, genomic data analysis, web search and engines, e. With more and more digital data available, it becomes clear that there are treasures of meaningful information buried in a data archive that is a very large and complex way for humans to understand. Learning to detect meaningful patterns in large and complex data sets is a promising field in which a set of programs that you learn with virtually unlimited memory capacity and accelerated processing speed of computers opens new horizons.

Adaptability, one of the limiting features of the program tools is their hardness - once the program has been written down and installed, it stays unchanged. However, many tasks change over time or from one user to another. Automated learning tools - Adaptive programs with input data - provide a solution to these issues.

By nature, they adapt to changes in the environment they interact with. Successful examples of automated learning of such problems include programs that decode handwritten text, where a fixed program can adapt to differences between handwriting for different users. Spam detection programs, automatic adaptation to changes in the nature of spam, and speech recognition programs.

Important tips for machine learning

In today's competitive world, every organization tries to outsmart its competitors in order to gain market share and improve the bottom line. They are constantly looking for new strategies and techniques in order to achieve this objective.

Machine learning is the new buzz word that has caught the attention of the organizations. Machine learning is a type of artificial intelligence that is related to the patterns and study of certain systems that use the huge input of data for its working. Here are the four things about this naive technique.

Complex pattern recognition - It has one of the most important features that it can be used to study and understand complex patterns in the data. It helps to give meaning to the data by providing a relationship and quantifying the same. This feature eliminates irrelevant data from the huge chunk of data and you are left with pure relevant data that can be used to dig out various useful insights. It also helps the user to understand primary and secondary variables for a set of information. This helps in the pre-processing technique and acceleration process.

Ability to take intelligent decisions - The process has the ability to take decisions with or without the guidance of a user. It is a type of artificial intelligence which makes decisions based on the input and the desired output. It selects the best optimum choice from a given set of options which will benefit the user as compared to the other

Self-Improving and Modifying: Suppose you teach in a Math class, who will you prefer as a student; a kid who makes the same mistake again and again or a kid who corrects his last mistake and improves next time? Your answer will more likely be the later one as it reduces your efforts by a great deal. Same is the case here. It has the characteristic of improving the standards of its decision-making ability and modifies itself for better, enhanced outputs benefit the user to a greater extent. It refines itself with multiple iterations on a particular problem and provides the user with an optimum solution.

Adds power to your analytics; Machine learning enhances the power of analytics. Consumer behavior is dynamic and changes constantly. It is important to tap and respond to these changes. It optimizes complex goals and improves lifetime value of the customers. It helps in building new predictive models in order to nullify the change. Another important characteristic is that it helps to track the process of a particular campaign right from the start of the campaign and not wait till the campaign ends.

CHAPTER TWO

Problems associated with Machine Learning

Machine Learning is one type of Artificial Intelligence (AI) that makes the computers to learn without being programmed explicitly.

It focuses on the development of computer programs that can change when exposed to new data.

Machine Learning tasks are classified into 3 categories, depending on the nature of learning signal or feedback of a learning system. They are as follows:

Supervised Learning: Here, the teacher gives example inputs and their desired outputs to the computer. The goal is to learn a rule that maps inputs to outputs.

Unsupervised Learning: Here nothing is given to the computer; the learning system itself has to find structure in its input. The goal is to discover hidden patterns in the data.

Reinforcement Learning: Here the computer program must perform a certain goal dynamically. The program gets feedback as rewards and punishments. These problems include,

Natural Language Processing: Understanding language is still a challenge for even the deepest networks.

Differential Neural Computers: These are a special type of memory augmented neural networks which can think but cannot scale.

Memory augmented neural networks are a type of neural networks which has memory blocks which can be read and written to by the network. We need to find the better way to discover facts, store and use them effectively to solve problems.

Object Detection: Machine Learning cannot understand or detect images.

Attention: Systems cannot grab attention in neural networks. So, we need to build attention mechanisms in neural networks to make them better.

Machine learning cannot learn by observations and listen.

One-shot learning: The ability to learn with fewer or fewer examples.

Effective Response Generation: The ability to generate contextual responses.

Automated learning from a repository of resources: Learning from other resources by making a graph connected sense.

Facial Identification over varying feature space: Facial recognition is not perfect even though it is a primary requirement.

How can you find the best machine learning for you?

You have to be very specific when you try to look forward to the perfect machine learning for you. If you have got any sort of worry then you have to ensure that right steps are taken as to find the best source that would prove to be the ultimate one for you. You have to look carefully at the different important services that you can find that would not make you get worried about any sort of reasons at all. This would bring a big smile of satisfaction to your face where it would not make you get tensed for any sort of reasons. Unless you make your best research it would prove to be very difficult to get the right one for you. Therefore your own important selection can help you to stay yourself on a much profitable side that would make you feel good of your own choice.

Have a look at their technology: You have to make sure that good efforts are taken to have a good look at their technology. This would help you to stay yourself assured of getting the right one for you. By having a good look at their technological innovation it would help you in a good way to anticipate the best one. It would prove to be the perfect one that would not let you get worried at all.

Ensure of looking at their services: It is also very important to look at their services that would make you get a clear picture of whether it would really be able to meet all your requirements. It is your own important selection where it would make you feel yourself good of your selection for the right attempt made by you in the right way. You can get all your doubts cleared that would help you to take your best decision without any worry at all. For this, you need to get in touch with them in the perfect way.

Check for the best solutions: You also need to find the best solutions that would make it possible to feel good about the right amount of steps that you have taken. It is therefore important to find the right one that would help you to provide with cognitive computing. This would help you in a good way to find the right amount of fulfilment.

What to Expect from a Machine Learning Engineer

If you have not had to deal with a Machine Learning Engineer, you obviously do not really know what sort of experience you will have when contacting such a professional to help you with your business. As you may probably know, nowadays, the best way of interacting with your target audience is with the help of artificial intelligence that analyzes live chat conversation data and provides instant solutions. The secret to success is a mix of human communication and the use of AI features.

Luckily there are some Machine Learning Engineers, who are working to constantly developing artificial intelligence system for commerce business's needs. When getting in touch with the company that can help your business succeed, you will want to first talk to an engineer and explain your problems and objectives. They will be able to guide you in the right direction and provide a personalized artificial intelligence product and be able to guide you in how it will make a difference in areas such as sales or customer retention. The Machine Learning Engineer will want to perform deep analysis of your live chat conversation data.

You should expect the Machine Learning Engineer, and the rest of the team to come up with a solution that will help you analyze the behavior of the individuals interested in your brand and teach your agents to communicate with them at a whole different level. There are just so many situations in which a few different words could have convinced the visitor to complete the purchase. But because of many quantifiable factors and the agent will not be able to personalize his answers according to social communication cues.

At the same time, it would be a mistake to replace your agents with catboats as customers do not really appreciate being approached by robots. In fact, the moment they realize that they are getting an automated response, they will decide to leave your website and opt for the assistance of your competitors. Obviously, this is something that you would like to avoid. It can be done up to the point where you will even get one step ahead of your competitors, but only if you invest in a different approach - artificial intelligence based training.

The interesting fact about the AI software is that it can be used with your current live chat system and it will ensure that your agents become more efficient at convincing visitors to complete their order and even buy other items that were not on their list. That is possible because the software will provide recommendations in real time after analyzing live chat conversation data. All feedback will be personalized according to the way in which the visitor communicates with your agent.

What are the steps used in Machine Learning?

There are 5 basic steps used to perform a machine learning task:

1. **Collecting data**: Be it the raw data from excel, access, text files etc., this step (gathering past data) forms the foundation of the future learning. The better the variety, density and volume of relevant data, better the learning prospects for the machine becomes.

2. **Preparing the data**: Any analytical process thrives on the quality of the data used. One needs to spend time determining the quality of data and then taking steps for fixing issues such as missing data and treatment of

outliers. Explanation analysis is perhaps one method to study the nuances of the data in details thereby burgeoning the nutritional content of the data.

3. **Training a model**: This step involves choosing the appropriate algorithm and representation of data in the form of the model. The cleaned data is split into two parts – train and test (proportion depending on the prerequisites); the first part (training data) is used for developing the model. The second part (test data), is used as a reference.

4. **Evaluating the model**: To test the accuracy, the second part of the data (holdout/test data) is used. This step determines the precision in the choice of the algorithm based on the outcome. A better test to check the accuracy of the model is to see its performance on data which was not used at all during model build.

5. **Improving the performance**: This step might involve choosing a different model altogether or introducing more variables to augment the efficiency. That's why a significant amount of time needs to be spent in data collection and preparation.

Be it any model, these 5 steps can be used to structure the technique and when we discuss the algorithms, you shall then find how these five steps appear in every model!

What's the Difference between Machine Learning Techniques?

AI and ML research has been around since computers existed. Of course, they allowed for practical creation and application. This challenge has always kept pace with the hype. Programmers were not usually able to do it - and so there were many "mistakes" of AI.

From a practical point of view, AI has basically got underground and provided everything from expert systems to behavioral vacuuming robots such as iRobot's Roomba. The other used an 8-bit microprocessor that used a behaviour-based rule system. Similarly, e-mail spam filters have been using Bayesian statistical techniques for decades, with varying levels of success.

AI is a very large area of research, whose machine learning is only one part (Figure 2). The three systems studied will be systems based on rules, Bayesian and statistical algorithms, and neural networks. These are described in more detail later. This list does not include more machine accesses.

1.   Systems based on rules and decision trees

Rule-based algorithms and decision trees are the easiest to understand. Rules-based systems consist of a set of logic rules or input-based conditions. The rule starts when its conditions are met. Running rules can change internal state variables as well as call origination.

For example, a robot can have several sensor inputs that detect touch barriers as well as motion inputs. The rule can cause the robot to stop when it moves and the obstacle sensor starts.

Rules can create conflicting actions in which a certain priority mechanism must be implemented. For example, one rule action can stop the robot, while another wants to change its direction.

A system based on rules or behavior usually moves from one country to another and applies all the rules for each state. It is not necessary to examine all the rules depending on the implementation. For example, rules can be grouped by inputs and some need to be reviewed only if input changes.

Decision trees are a structure-based system where each node in a tree has conditions that allow grading by refining as the algorithm passes through the tree. There are many popular algorithms in this area, including CART and Chi-squared automatic detection interaction

2. Bayesian and statistics

The Bayes Theorem describes the likelihood of a test result based on previous knowledge of conditions that may be related to the result. This sentence is related to the probability that event A has happened with the X, $\Pr(A \mid X)$ indicator of event X probability given by A, $\Pr(X \mid A)$, allows correction of measurement errors if real probabilities are known. Of course, the test results come with the probability of the test.

There are several Bayesian tree-based algorithms, including Naive Byes and Bayesian Belief Network (BBN). Like differential equations, the theory can be difficult to understand, but the application is usually simple. As noted above, Bayes algorithms have been used in applications such as email spam filtering, but are not limited to this narrow application.

Bayes is just one method that uses probability and statistics. There are also regression algorithms that have been used in machine learning. Popular regression algorithms include least squares regression (OLSR), multidimensional regression spline (MARS) and, of course, linear regression.

There are also regression variants that are used in machine learning, such as ridge regression. It is also known as weight loss. It is also known as the Tikhon-Miller method and the Phillips-Twomey method. Variants try to simplify models to reduce the complexity of the system that provides better support for generalization.

3.   Neural Networks

Artificial neural networks (ANNs) have been in place for a long time, but their high computational requirements for complex networks have limited the use and experimentation until recently of multi-core systems such as GPGPUs that provide an economic platform for variants called deep neural networks (DNNs)

Initially, neural networks were interesting as a way of copying biological neuronal networks such as the human brain. The brain is formed by neurons that are connected through the axon to synapses and dendrites on other neurons. Electrical signals from incoming signals are summarized by the neuron. The result that exceeds the threshold value sends a signal through the axon.

ANNs are built in a similar way, but using electronics or software. It took many neurons to perform useful functions; the human brain has 100 billion. The trick that it has something useful is the way the neurons are connected, as well as the weights associated with neurons.

The basic neural network consists of a set of hidden-layer inputs and outputs (Figure 3). DNN has several hidden layers. Networks can be the same logically, but the number of inputs, outputs, and hidden layers is different as well as other configuration options.

CHAPTER THREE

MACHINE LEARNING IN PRACTICE

How machine learning personalization adds to your bottom line

Lift Igniter is a personalization developer app that works by showing the content that your visitors want to see. More articles are recommended based upon what your visitor is interested in. This leads to higher conversions and greater click through rates. This is an excellent way to improve the bounce rate on your articles and videos. This personalization AI also works by recommending videos to visitors that they would like to see at the right time. You can monetize the clicks and views on your app or website using this technology.

When content is personalized to the viewer, they will stay on your site longer. There is a multitude of useful features including showing a specific set of content to a certain set of users. You can also show specific content for a certain amount of time, depending on who your visitor is. Publishers understand that not every visitor is going to be interested in the same content. So it's in your best interest to only show the content that each particular user likes. This would normally be a difficult task, but personalization AI makes it an easy task that is done automatically.

Machine learning personalization is a highly effective way to deliver content that satisfies while also monetizing it. You can help your visitor quickly understand that your site has what they're looking for. By offering high-level product discovery, you create a more pleasant shopping experience. Having a website that reacts personally to each visitor is priceless. By using state-of-the-art personalization, you're utilizing technology on the same caliber as Google and Amazon. Your website or app is far more dynamic when it's able to place the ideal content in front of each individual user.

Lift Igniter is the way to show quality content to your visitors every time, avoiding links that are designed to be click bait. It wouldn't be appropriate to say that this is the way of the future since this is the technology that many companies are utilizing today. Links and content suggestions should change from visitor to visitor, as each one is different.

You can expect to increase your click through rates anywhere from 50% to 80% by utilizing this technology on your site or app. Serving up better product recommendations is definitely going to equal more money for your bottom line. Every e-commerce site that's not using a personalization developer app is at a tremendous loss.

If you're looking for more engagement and conversions, consider how this machine learning technology can help your business. Lift Igniter will always choose the right content because it updates in real time based on impressions. You'll never have to play the guessing game of trying to figure out what your visitors are interested in. Your visitors will get the right piece of content right away.

Ways AI Is Already Making a Difference in Society

By now, everyone and their grandparents are talking about machine learning and AI. Unfortunately, many people have been questioning whether all this effort is worth it, and some are worried about future job losses.

Machine learning can offer real-world value. The increased ease, speed, and functionality it offers create avenues for use cases across the spectrum of industries that rely heavily on data.

For retail businesses, it provides an opportunity to improve and customize the customer experience. Let's take a look at five examples that are worth noting.

1. Machine learning helping the disabled

Much like the closed captioning we've seen on TV, machine learning now makes it possible to identify specific elements from YouTube videos. New algorithms can visualize sound effects like applause, laughter, and music. This is a huge development for the versatility of the platform as it looks to become more accessible. Google's new video intelligence API made big news recently at Google Cloud Next, and it uses extremely high-tech models to identify specific elements in the video. This can include things as descriptive as a smile, water, or a species of animal. Machine learning makes these possible, and it opens the door for many new advances that will make online content more accessible for the disabled. Considering the amount of new content being developed that emphasizes audio-visual interactivity, this is a huge breakthrough for the disabled.

2. Suicide prevention

After some horrific events involving the live streaming of suicides, Facebook garnered a considerable amount of negative feedback. To combat the issue, the company decided to implement machine learning capabilities in the fight to prevent suicide. Machine learning will now "build predictive models to tailor interventions earlier." It's coming at the right time, considering there's been an increase in suicide rates over the past couple of years. With appropriate data mining, Facebook and others will be able to identify suicidal tendencies earlier and will be able to intervene more quickly.

3. Wearable medical devices

A company called Geneia is using machine learning to increase data efficiency and improve insights. By better-utilizing data, Geneia is able to improve medical status predictions at a much quicker rate. This means responses arrive earlier and contribute to a higher quality of care. Clinical assessments and lab values used in the past are much less speedy and efficient. As a result of machine learning, there's a very real possibility that the sick or elderly can live more comfortably at home while reducing many of the risks associated with being away from medical facilities.

4. Student growth measures for success

Anyone who's studied in a public classroom knows that there are a number of different learning styles. Not everyone's brain functions the same, and everyone has different needs. Thanks to machine learning, meeting those needs is becoming much easier. Use of student-level projections allows for a standardized measure of success so that each student can learn and progress according to their own characteristics. This creates a much higher chance for a student to respond positively and ultimately gives that student a better chance of learning.

5. Machine learning identifying skin cancer

Stanford researchers have been working very hard on this one. They've created a machine learning algorithm that uses a massive image database to make skin cancer diagnoses. Using the more recent developments combining deep learning with visual identification, the algorithm is aimed at replacing the initial observation step of skin cancer diagnosis.

This will make the process easier and more efficient for both the patient and the doctor. Though the algorithm currently exists on a computer, there's a plan in place to expand to mobile very soon.

When you look at some of these cases, it's clear that there's a lot more at stake when we talk about the value of machine learning. Most of the buzzworthy tech news falls short of providing a sense of the huge potential at stake. Though current uses may seem simplistic, they are simply building blocks to begin using the technology in much more widespread, impactful ways.

How Machine Learning Influences Your Productivity

If there is a word with which the company wants to be associated, it is "productive". This is the measure that influences so many others whose businesses are a measured success, efficiency, profit, and recently, Artificial Intelligence (AI) was seen as a new way to increase productivity by replacing expensive workers with tireless machines. A recent example that attracted the attention of the media is the first demonstration of a large stand-alone platform, the use of which could replace millions of truckers.

But AI has received many underserved projections. Long before the machines replace us, humans, they will help us make smart decisions so we can become more productive, this use of technology is called "increased intelligence" and, because of its imminent and extensive impact, it deserves a closer look.

For many in the business, artificial intelligence (AI) versus increasing intelligence (AI) is a distinction without a difference. And certainly, this case can be made. In a Wall Street Journal article, IBM President, President and CEO Ginni Rometty points out that, whether you call AI or IA, "these cognitive systems are neither autonomous nor sensitive, but they form a new type of" Intelligence that has nothing artificial about it. They increase our ability to understand what is happening in the complex world that surrounds us.

This is absolutely true. But there is still a distinction to be made when maximizing productivity in the modern and diverse workplace. The application of either technology to the wrong task will be counterproductive, even if the application could be advanced.

The "intelligence" provided by AI technology involves taking advantage of increasingly costly computer processing power to evaluate other options faster than humans. That's why AI-controlled computers have managed to play chess, win at Go, and even play at Jeopardy. Each of these tasks is characterized by the need to evaluate the best move from a finite set of options, although the number of options may be large. Assessing many options and learning from past experience - using a technology called machine learning - is whether artificial intelligence is able to choose the best outcome available.

But business decisions involve more than evaluating many options. Business decisions involve ethics and intangibles, things that computers cannot explain. This is where humans come. And that's what's so convincing for the AI. It allows humans to direct computers to evaluate options and then suggest suggestions on what to do next. It is this type of cooperation between man and machine that will bring humanity to the next level of productivity.

How does this work?

A practical example of exploiting machine intelligence to increase humans in a daily economic scenario is to gather disparate information from a wide variety of applications and then to use intelligence enhancement technologies, Such as natural language processing and machine learning, in order to automatically combine the associated information. This could mean collecting information from Salesforce, Dropbox, e-mail, Office 365, Workday and many other applications, and then collecting related information in an ecological way in all applications so that a human can see the forest Information rather than getting lost in the data trees. This is an incredibly taxable cognitive process for humans, but simple for smart machines. With all the related information presented in a coherent context, the human can then make intelligent decisions about what to do next.

This does not mean that AI will supplant the AI. Every use of intelligent technology has its place. Cases such as the use of caterers to replace human operators will become more common. Today, you can order food from Taco Bell via Slack or a pizza from Domino robots. These robots manage the types of tasks that AI can manage more effectively than a person because the context is clearly defined and the degree of decision-making is extremely limited.

It's when the context becomes ambiguous, the decision criteria become fuzzy, and ethical considerations must be taken into consideration that AI falls short. It's here that intelligence augmentation can help people by presenting information and options in a coherent manner and letting the human take it from there. This is how machine intelligence will truly help organizations and individuals become more productive in the near- to mid-term, so this is where enterprises should be focused.

While artificial intelligence can improve efficiency by replacing humans for focused tasks, it is in the application of machine intelligence to augment human decision-making that the real increase in business productivity will occur. Understanding the roles machine learning can play is the key to maximizing both artificial and human intelligence in the enterprise.

How Machine Learning Is Improving Companies Work Processes

Machine learning allows companies to expand their top-line growth and optimize processes while improving employee engagement and increasing customer satisfaction. Here are some concrete examples of how AI and machine learning create value in today's business:

Customized customer service: The potential to improve customer service while reducing costs makes it one of the most attractive areas of opportunity. By combining historical customer service data, natural language processing and algorithms that continually learn from interactions, customers can ask questions and get high-quality responses. Customer service representatives can intervene to handle exceptions, algorithms that explore their shoulders to learn how to do next time.

Improve customer retention and loyalty: Companies can exploit customer actions, transactions and social sentiment data to identify customers who are at risk of leaving. Combined with profitability data, organizations can optimize "next best action" strategies and customize the end-to-end customer experience. For example, young adults who leave mobile phone projects from their parents often move to other carriers. They can use machine learning to anticipate this behavior and make customized offers, depending on the individual's usage patterns, before they are defective to competitors.

Hire the right people: The software quickly spends thousands of work applications and small list candidates who possess the credentials most likely to succeed at the company. Care must be taken not to reinforce the human bias implicit in the previous hiring. But software can also combat human bias by automatically signalling biased language in job descriptions, detecting highly skilled candidates who might have been neglected because they did not meet traditional expectations.

Finance Automation: AI can expedite the handling of exceptions in many financial processes. For example, when a payment is received without an order number, a person must settle the payment voucher and determine what to do with an excess or loss of earnings. By monitoring existing processes and learning to recognize different situations, AI dramatically increases the number of bills that can correspond automatically. This allows organizations to reduce the amount of outsourced work in service centers and free up the finance staff to focus on strategic tasks.

Measure Brand Exposure: Automated programs can recognize products, people, logos and more. For example, advanced image recognition can be used to track the position of brand logos that appear in video footage of a sporting event, such as a basketball game. Corporate sponsors see the return on investment of their investment by sponsoring with detailed analysis, including the quantity, duration, and placement of company logos.

Fraud Detection: By building models based on historical transactions, social network information, and other external sources of data, automated learning algorithms can be used to identify spot pattern abnormalities, exceptions, and extreme values. This helps to detect and prevent fraudulent transactions in real time, even for unknown types of fraud previously. For example, banks can use historical transaction data to build algorithms that recognize phishing behavior. They can also detect suspicious patterns of payments and transfers between networks of individuals with overlapping contacts with companies. This type of "security algorithm" applies to a wide range of situations, such as cyber security and tax evasion.

Predictive Maintenance: Automatic learning makes it possible to detect anomalies at the temperature of the train axis indicating that they will freeze in the next few hours. Instead of hundreds of passengers trapped in the countryside, waiting for costly repair, the train can be converted to maintenance before its failure, and passengers are taken to another train.

Seamless supply chains: Allows automated learning of contextual analysis of logistic data to predict and mitigate supply chain risk. Algorithms can be penetrated through general social data and news feeds in multiple languages to detect, for example, a fire in a remote plant that provides dynamic ball bearings that are used to transport the vehicle.

Other areas where the intelligence service may be commonly used include:

Career Planning: Recommendations can help staff to choose career paths that lead to high performance, satisfaction, and retention. If someone who has an engineering degree wants to manage the department someday, what additional education and practical experience should they receive, and in what order?

Unmanned aircraft and satellite assets management: Unmanned drones can carry out regular external inspections of commercial structures, such as bridges or aircraft, with automatic image analysis to detect any new cracks or changes to surfaces.

Retail store analysis: A sports drink company can use the automated intelligence, along with the machine vision, to see if the display screens in the store at the promised location, and the shelves are stored properly with the products, and face the product labels out.

Automated learning enables the company to re-visualize end-to-end business processes with digital intelligence. This is why software vendors are investing heavily in adding AI to their current applications and in creating new solutions. But there are barriers that must be overcome.

Most important is the availability of large amounts of high-quality data that can be used to train algorithms. In many organizations, data is not in one place or in usable form, or it contains biases that will lead to bad decisions. To prepare your project for the future, the first step is to evaluate current information systems and data flows to identify areas that are ready to automate those that need more investment. Consider hiring a senior data officer to ensure that the data is properly managed as an asset for the company.

Another problem is prioritizing; with lots of opportunities, it can be hard to know where to start. To facilitate this burden, software providers have begun to offer pre-defined enabling solutions with state-of-the-art learning machines from outside the box. Many organizations also implement Amnesty International's centers of excellence to work closely with business administrations. Wherever it started, it is important to link projects with a long-term digital platform strategy to avoid islands of innovation.

Finally, do not underestimate the cultural barriers. Many employees are concerned about the consequences of all this technology on their roles. For most, it will be an opportunity to reduce tedious tasks and do more, but it is important that employees have incentives to ensure the success of new learning initiatives. You will also have to think carefully about customers. AI can increase the ability to obtain insights from customer data - perhaps beyond the point where customers are comfortable.

Organizations must take privacy very seriously; relying on computers to make important decisions requires careful management. They should implement procedures to review the real effects of any automated systems, and there should always be resources and overruns as part of the operations. Artificial intelligence systems using data on persons should include informed consent.

In conclusion, the continued rise of Amnesty International is inevitable, and it is progressing to the workplace with amazing speed. The question now is not whether managers should investigate AI's adoption but how fast they can do it. At the same time, organizations need to be well informed about how Amnesty International applies to their organizations, with a full understanding of the inherent advantages and disadvantages of technology.

CHAPTER FOUR

MACHINE LEARNING FUNCTIONS

Learning Input-Output Functions

To help define some of the terminology used in describing the problem of learning a function. Imagine that there is a function, f, and the task of the learner is to guess what it is. Our hypothesis about the function to be learned is denoted by h. Both f and h are functions of a vector-valued input $X = (x1, x2 \ldots xi \ldots xn)$ which has n components. We think of h as being implemented by a device that has X as input and h(X) as output. Both f and h themselves may be vector-valued. We assume that the hypothesized function, h, is selected from a class of functions H. Sometimes we know that f also belongs to this class or to a subset of this class. We select h based on a training set, of m input vector examples. Many important details depend on the nature of the assumptions made about all of these entities.

Input Vectors

Because machine learning methods derive from so many different traditions, For example, the input vector is called by a variety of names. Some of these are input vector, pattern vector, the feature vector, sample, example, and instance. The components, xi, of the input vector are variously called features, attributes, input variables, and components.

The values of the components can be of three main types. They might be real-valued numbers, discrete-valued numbers, or categorical values. As an example illustrating categorical values, information about a student might be represented by the values of the attributes class, major, sex, and adviser. A particular student would then be represented by a vector such as: (sophomore, history, male, Higgins).

Additionally, categorical values may be ordered (as in {small, medium, large}) or unordered (as in the example just given). Of course, mixtures of all these types of values are possible. In all cases, it is possible to represent the input in unordered form by listing the names of the attributes together with their values. The vector form assumes that the attributes are ordered and given implicitly by a form. As an example of an attribute-value representation, we might have: (major: history, sex: male, class: sophomore, adviser: Higgins, age: 19).

An important specialization uses Boolean values, which can be regarded as a special case of either discrete numbers (1, 0) or of categorical variables (True, False)

Outputs

The output may be a real number, in which case the process embodying the function, h, is called a function estimator, and the output is called an output value or estimate. Alternatively, the output may be a categorical value, in which case the process embodying h is variously called a classifier, a recognizer, or a categorizer, and the output itself is called a label, a class, a category, or a decision. Classic- fires have application in a number of recognition problems, for example in the recognition of hand-printed characters. The input, in that case, is some suitable representation of the printed character, and the classifier maps, this input into one of, say, 64 categories. Vector-valued outputs are also possible with components being real numbers or categorical values. An important special case is that of Boolean output values. In that case, a training pattern having value 1 is called a positive instance, and a training sample having value 0 is called a negative instance. When the input is also Boolean, the classifier implements a Boolean function. Learning a Boolean function is sometimes called concept learning, and the function is called a concept

Training Regimes

There are several ways in which the training set can be used to produce a hypothesized function. In the batch method, the entire training set is available and used all at once to compute the function, h. A variation of this method uses the entire training set to modify a current hypothesis iteratively until an acceptable hypothesis is obtained. By contrast, in the incremental method, we select one member at a time from the training set and use this instance alone to modify a current hypothesis. Then another member of the training set is selected, and so on. The selection method can be random (with replacement) or it can cycle through the training set iteratively. If the entire training set becomes available one member at a time, then we might also use an incremental method selecting and using training set members as they arrive.

(Alternatively, at any stage all training set members so far available could be used in a "batch" process.) Using the training set members as they become available is called an online method. Online methods might be used, for example, when the next training instance is some function of the current hypothesis and the previous instance—as it would be when a classifier is used to decide on a robot's next action given its current set of sensory inputs. The next set of sensory inputs will depend on which action was selected.

Not everything is Learnable

Although machine learning works well, perhaps astonishingly well in many cases, it is important to keep in mind that it is not magical. There are many reasons why a machine learning algorithm might fail on some learning task. There could be noise in the training data. Noise can occur both at the feature level and at the label level. Some features might correspond to measurements taken by sensors.

For instance, a robot might use a laser range finder to compute its distance to a wall. However, this sensor might fail and return an incorrect value. In a sentiment classification problem, someone might have a typo in their review of a course. These would lead to noise at the feature level. There may also be noise at the label level. A student might write a contemptuously negative review of a course, but then accidentally click the wrong button for the course rating. The features available for learning might simply be insufficient. For example, in a medical context, you might wish to diagnose whether a patient has cancer or not. You may be able to collect a large amount of data about this patient, such as gene expressions, X-ray, Family history, etc. However, even knowing all this information exactly, it may still be impossible to judge for sure whether this patient has cancer or not.

As a more open example, you may try to classify session reviews as positive or negative. But you may have made a mistake when loading the data and got only the first five characters of each review. If you have the rest of the features you may be able to do a good job. But with this limited feature set, there is not much you can do. Some examples may not have a single correct answer. You can create a system for Safe Search on the web, which removes offensive web pages from search results. To build this system, you can collect a collection of web pages and ask people to classify them as "offensive" or not. However, what an offensive person considers to be quite reasonable may be someone else's. It is common to consider this as a form of a nuisig label. However, because of you, as a designer of the learning system, have some control over this problem; it is sometimes helpful to isolate it as a source of difficulty.

Finally, learning may fail because the inductive bias of the learning algorithm is far from the concept being learned. In bird/non bird data, you may think that if you've got a few more training examples, you might be able to tell if this was intended to be a bird / non-bird classification or a fly/non-flying classification. Even with many training points, this is such an unusual distinction that it may be difficult for anyone to find out. In this case, the inductive bias of the learner is simply not very aligned with the target classification of learning. Note that the source of the bias error is fundamentally different from the other three sources of error.

In the case of inductive bias, it is the special learning algorithm you use that cannot handle the data. Maybe if you switch to a different learning algorithm, you will be able to learn well. For example, Neptune and may have evolved into great care about whether the backgrounds are in focus, and for them, this will be easy to classify for learning. For the other three sources of error, it is not a problem to be done with a particular learning algorithm

The Importance of Good Features

The Importance of Good Features Learning by machine is magical. You give him data and he can sort that out. For many, it can actually surpass a human! But, like so many problems in the world, there is an important aspect of garbage disposal in machine learning. If the data you give is a waste, it is unlikely that the learning algorithm can overcome it. Consider a problem of object recognition from images. If you start with a 100 × 100-pixel image, a very simple feature representation of that image is a dimensional vector of 30,000, each dimension corresponding to the red, green, or blue component of some pixels in the image. So maybe feature 1 is the amount of red in pixels (1, 1); Characteristic 2 is the amount of green in this pixel; etc.

This is the pixel representation of the images. Object Recognition in Pixels One thing to keep in mind is that the pixel representation throws all the locality information into the image. Learning algorithms do not care about functionality: they only care about functionality values. So you can swap all features without affecting the learning algorithm. All these objects are things of which you have seen many examples.

An alternative representation of the images is the representation of the patch, where the unit of interest is a small rectangular block of an image rather than a single pixel. Again, swapping patches has no effect on the classifier. A final representation is a representation of form. Here, we throw all the information about colours and pixels and simply provide a delimiting polygon. In the context of the categorization of the text (for example, the task of feeling recognition), a standard representation is the sign of the representation of the words. Here we have a feature for each single word that appears in a document. For the functionality to be happy, the value of the function is the number of times the word "happy" appears in the document.

CHAPTER FIVE

How edge computing and server less deliver scalable machine learning services

Machine learning, computing and server less are the three major technologies that will redefine the cloud computing platforms.

Machine learning (ML) has become an integral world's part of modern applications. From the Internet to mobile phone to Internet stuff, ML is generating a new breed of applications through natural user experiences and inbuilt intelligence.

After virtualization and continuation, surfers are emerging as the next wave of account services. Servers or Service-as-a-Service (FAS) attempts to simplify the developer's experience by reducing operational costs in deploying and managing code. Contemporary applications that are designed as micro services are built on top of Fes platforms such as OSA Lambda, Azure functions, Google Cloud functions, and Open Whysk.

The edge of computing takes account closer to applications. Each site simulates the general cloud edge by exposing a consistent set of services and points that applications can consume. It is scheduled to redefine the Foundation's infrastructure.

These three emerging technologies - server less computing, computing and learning machine will be the main technology drivers for the next generation of infrastructure. The aim of this book is to explain how developers will benefit from combining these technologies.

Data availability, ample storage capacity, and adequate computing capacity are necessary to implement Machine Learning. Cloud becomes a natural fit to handle the learning machine. Data Scientists rely on the cloud to accommodate and store large data sets. It also uses the pay-as-you-go infrastructure to process and analyze data. With cheaper storage and advanced computing platforms powered by GPUs and Vegas, the cloud quickly turns into a destination for building complex ML models.

At a high level, there are three steps involved in building applications based on ML. The first stage is to train an algorithm with existing data. The second stage is to validate the result for accuracy with the test data. These steps are repeated until the expected accuracy is achieved by the algorithm. With each repetition, the algorithm learns more about the data and finds new patterns, which will increase efficiency. What comes out of these two steps is the Machine learning model, which is carefully tuned to work with new data points. The third and final step is based on the model with production data to achieve the expected result, which can be based on forecasting, classification or aggregation of new data.

The first two phases, which involve multiple molluscs, require a heavy lifting, which is treated by the cloud. Training and testing data is stored in cloud storage, while a special class of virtual machines is used to set the algorithm. An interesting fact is that the final model, evolved from the ML does not need too many resources. Is a piece of code that contains the parameters obtained from the previous two stages based on rigorous training and validation. For many scenarios, this form can be included in an application as a separate entity. Based on predefined parameters, it will analyze the new data points as they get generated. When the production data set submitted to the model becomes significantly different than expected, the need for retraining of the algorithm arises. At this point, a new model is developed after repeated testing and training phases. The updated application model is then redistributed to process the production data sets.

From the operations point of view, generating ML models requires providing and configuring a variety of storage and resource calculation. Divubbs teams are involved in managing the infrastructure needed for this task. The operations team will have to ensure that the evolving model is delivered to the applications. Each model can be tracked and maintained through the issuing mechanism. Finally, the model should be available to developers who consume it in their applications. This is where the Surfless platforms play a vital role in streamlining the DevOps cycle.

Although the Machine learning model is created in the cloud, it may not be called in the cloud. For most scenarios, the model should be kept close to applications. For example, a predictive maintenance model created to detect a bug in a connected car needs to be closer to the cars than running in the cloud. These models are usually pushed to the edge of the cloud computing layer. Like the Content Delivery Network (KDN), which stores hard content and video streams across multiple points of presence, an ML model must be hosted across multiple sites within an edge network. Applications will call the ML model closest to its location. This reduces dormancy by avoiding round trip back to the cloud. Since DevOps teams are responsible for pushing the latest ML model across multiple edge sites, they can automate the process of upgrading the model.

At each edge location, the ML model is deployed as a Server less function, which is invoked by applications. Since the unit of deployment in FaaS is a function, it is far more efficient than pushing a heavy virtual machine or a container. Each time a new ML model is evolved; a new version is assigned to it and pushed across all the locations. This makes the process less error prone and efficient.

To summarize, while the heavy lifting for ML will be done in the cloud, the edge layer will simplify the deployment experience, and Server less will streamline the developer experience.

Unconventional knowledge about machine learning that you can't learn from books

Ever since Sci-Fi movies having robots who could think of their own were screened, people have mused over the possibility of interacting with such machines and robots that have the capacity to do smart work. We may not realize it yet, but we are already surrounded by such machines which are performing smart actions and taking decisions comparable with the human cognitive process.

Days of having R2-D2 as your companion may still be a few years away, but we are already surrounded by machines that are taking smart decisions and interacting with each other to make our lives easier. Machine learning is currently an area of immense study, and a large number of books and study materials are available which provide knowledge of Machine Learning. Also, some Machine Learning courses are available offline and online which provides comprehensive training in the domain. These Machine Learning courses will also provide you with certain unique features of the domain which you may not be able to find in books. Let's check out some unconventional knowledge about Machine Learning that you won't come across in any books except this:

1. Concentrate on feature engineering!

Imagine a given data set from which you have to create an algorithm to create certain outputs by which certain decisions will be made. For example, imagine a data set containing the specific times when each employee enters the office, leaves for lunch, comes back and leaves for home. By these, we have to find out the employee who spends the most time in office and award him/her the best employee award. But, the specific times or a pair of specific times or so will not be able to provide enough data to create an algorithm for this. Now, if you can create a new data set which contains the summation of time duration which the employee spends in office between coming and going for lunch and then coming back from lunch and going to the office, we can easily create an algorithm to test the said condition. This is known as feature engineering and the maximum time is to be spent on this in order to create better algorithms which are flexible and require lesser bug fixing.

2. More data and a simpler algorithm is better than a complicated clever algorithm

It is a proven fact that once the input fields are defined, there is only a limited amount of analytic variations that you can perform with the algorithm. Having a simpler algorithm with a better flexibility for addition and variation along with a large data set is always beneficial to create incredibly powerful classifiers with increasing data load.

3. Learn variations in models

Learn multiple classifiers with random data subsets to create more powerful models of machine learning. There is a possibility that there is a little loss in interpretability due to the varying sequence in models for the final prediction, but making the application performance sensitive will increase your power to compensate for the loss of interpretability.

4. Do not be oversimplified at the cost of accuracy

To quote Occam's razor, "plurality is not to be posited without necessity." In simpler terms, if a particular problem has two solutions, the simpler one is more effective. In machine learning, however, this hypothesis should not be used extensively. At many places in machine learning, algorithms with additional complexity can benefit with more performance. In short, prefer simple models for their ease and quickness of fitting along with better interpretability but never be blind enough to be sure that they will lead to better performance.

5. Correlation does not necessarily mean causation

When modeling observable data, the correlation between two variables can come out to be definite, but this will not necessarily tell us 'why?' And until you know the 'why' you cannot conclude a causative relation. Just because it is visualized that the presence of one thing is also in the presence of another thing, it does not mean the presence of the thing is because of the other thing. Machine learning will go a long way in changing the technological world in ways we cannot imagine right now. Organizations are now considering machine learning as their core research areas and the next 'internet' of the future. Getting trained in machine learning through books or Machine Learning courses will go a long way in sky rocketing individual's careers.

Hardware alternative for ML and AI quantum computing

Quantum computing continues to expand with the recent announcement from the Vancouver-based quantum computing company, D-Wave, of its 2,000 kubit processing, it does not show signs of slowing down. D-Wave is the first quantum computing company that has made technology available for commercial use. Quantum computing processors are in competition with more conventional types of chips used for machine learning and AI-like GPUs and newly announced second-generation TPU from Google.

The important part of quantum computing is that it replaces the traditional way of thinking about computing. By replacing the traditional bit, 0 or 1, with a new type of information, it opens up to exponential amounts of possibilities. Coppet can be in an overlay condition where it does neither +1 nor -1 after, meaning it is both that allows for ultrafast computing.

D-Wave quantum computers are used in the process of mating. This involves a series of microscopic magnetism to be arranged on the grid. Each magnetic field affects each other, and then directs itself to the position to reduce the amount of energy stored in the entire field. Through this process, one can change the magnetic field strength of each magnet so that the magnet guides them in a way to solve specific problems. To reach the solution, you have to start with high amounts of energy, so it is easy to magnet the face back and forth. Then as you lower the temperature, the magnets reach lower levels and less energy until they are frozen in the lowest power state. Here it is possible to read the direction of each magnet and find the answer to the problem. One can say that quantum computer D-Wave is a type of computer measuring relying on nature's algorithms in finding the configuration of the lowest power state.

This is where we get luck. This category of qualitative quantum computing speaks to be useful for a subset of optimization computing problems, especially those geared towards automated learning. Many machine learning problems can rework energy problems. D-Wave quantum computers are designed to support problems that need a high level of thinking followed by decision-making. Quantum computing allows AI systems to mimic human thought processes much more closely than classical treatments. The idea of quantum computing can be difficult to understand, its use in machine learning opens up new opportunities.

In the impending battle between GPUs and TBIs, there is a possibility that quantum computing will pass through the outer aisle. A key element of quantum computing D-Wave is that it is not necessarily designed to solve every problem but addresses the same need in the processing market currently performed by GPUs. Google released a paper that they found that there is a great computational advantage when using quantum computer D-Wave above the classic processor.

CHAPTER SIX

MACHINE LEARNING FOR DATA SCIENCE AND ANALYTICS

Importance of Algorithm in programming, AI, and machine lemming

Algorithm: This is no longer an unknown term for many of us, and today algorithms exist in all aspects of computing. Algorithms are widely used in various top-level domains such as social media, e-commerce, transportation, healthcare, education, etc. With increasing technological trends, today's algorithms are considered key elements of machine learning (ML) and artificial intelligence (AI).

An algorithm, in general, is a sequence of instructions, which ultimately confirms the success of a specific task. Being human, we apply algorithms to perform certain actions in all aspects of our daily life.

The algorithm allows us to break something in small steps, for an easy and effective understanding of complex things. For example, in the morning when you are ready to go to the office and you cannot remember where the keys of the car are, how would you find them? A smart approach could be the application of an algorithm, which is a sequential procedure to quickly locate the answer (keys). In the beginning, you will see the places where you usually deposit the keys. Then you will remember the last opportunity when you used them. Later, you will check the first room where you went, when entering the house. Finally, by the passage of the steps, you will find the keys to the car. Thus, knowledge of the algorithm must be a valuable asset in enlightening our everyday life or even the lives of others. With the algorithms, there is no limit to imagine and make them real.

Advantages of using Algorithms

There are many advantages of using algorithms in our personal and professional lives, some of them are explained below.

You can turn any complicated thing into an algorithm that will help you in the decision-making process.

Instead of creating a to-do list, you should write an algorithm to prioritize your daily tasks.

Depending on your preferences and historical data, you can write an algorithm to get recommendations on genre films to watch for.

The Algorithms machine learning Engineers need to know

There is no doubt that the sub-field of machine learning / artificial intelligence has gained increasing popularity in recent years. As Big Data is the hottest trend in the technology industry at the moment, machine learning is incredibly powerful in making predictions or suggestions calculated based on large amounts of data. Some of the most common examples of machine learning are the Netflix algorithms to make movie suggestions based on movies you've watched in the past or Amazon algorithms that recommend books based on books you have already purchased.

So, if you want to learn more about machine learning, how can you start?

The automatic learning algorithms can be divided into 3 main categories: supervised learning, unsupervised learning, and enhanced learning. Supervised learning is useful in cases where a property (label) is available for a certain set of data (training set) but is missing and must be predicted for other instances. Unsupervised learning is useful in cases where the challenge is to discover implicit relationships in a given unmarked dataset (the elements are not pre-assigned). The reinforcement learning lies between these two extremes: there is a form of feedback available for each step or predictive action, but no precise label or error message.

Supervised Learning

1. **Decision shrubs**: A decision tree is a decision-making tool that uses a graph or decision model in a tree structure and their possible consequences, including the results of unforeseen events, resource costs, and utility. From a business decision point of view, a decision tree is the minimum number of yes / no questions that need to be asked, to assess the likelihood of making a correct decision, most of the time. As a method, it allows you to approach the problem in a structured and systematic way to arrive at a logical conclusion.

2. **Naïve Bayes Classification**: Naïve Bayes classifiers are a family of simple probabilistic classifiers based on the application of the Bayes theorem with strong (naïve) assumptions of independence between the characteristics. $P(A)$ is a later probability, $P(B \mid A)$ is a likelihood, $P(A)$ is a previous probability of class, and $P(B)$ is a probability Predictive anterior.

Some examples of the real world are:

- To mark an e-mail as spam or no spam
- Classify an article on technology, politics or sport
- Check a piece of text expressing positive emotions or negative emotions?
- Used for facial recognition software.

3. **Ordinary least squares regression**: If you know the statistics, you probably already heard of linear regression. The least square is a method to perform a linear regression. You can think of linear regression as a task of aligning a straight line across a set of points. There are several possible strategies to do this, and the "ordinary least squares" strategy goes like this: you can draw a line and then, for each of the data points, measure the vertical distance between the point and the line and add them; The adjusted line would be that where this sum of distances is as small as possible.
Linear refers to the type of model you are using to match the data, while the least squares refer to the type of error measurement you are minimizing.

4. **Logistic Regression**: It is a powerful statistical method of modeling a binomial result with one or more explanatory variables. It measures the relationship between the categorical dependent variable and one or more independent variables by estimating the probabilities using a logistic function, which is the cumulative logistic distribution.

- Credit rating
- Measure success rates of marketing campaigns

- Forecast revenue for a certain product
- Will there be an earthquake on any given day?
    5. **Support Vector Machines**: SVM is a binary classification algorithm. Given a set of points of 2 types in dimensional N, SVM generates a dimensional hyperplane (N-1) to separate these points into two groups. Let's say you have a few points of 2 types in a document that is separable linearly. SVM will find a straight line that separates these points into two types and is located as far as possible from all these points. Regarding scale, some of the major problems that have been solved using SVM (with appropriately modified implementations) are display advertising, human splicing sites recognition, gender-based detection Image, and classification of large-scale images .
    6. **Ensemble Methods**: Ensemble methods are learning algorithms that construct a set of classifiers and then classify the new data points by taking a weighted vote of their predictions. The original set method is the Bayesian average, but more recent algorithms include output coding, bagging and error amplification.

So how do the overall methods work and why are they superior to individual models?

- They exceed prejudices: if you count together a series of democratic polls and Republican polls, you will get an average that does not rely on any way.
- They reduce variance: the overall opinion of a set of models is less noisy than the one opinion of one of the models. In finance, this is called diversification - a mixed portfolio of many stocks will be much less

variable than one of the stocks alone. This is why your models will be better with more data points than less.

- It is unlikely to be too good: if you have individual models that do not go too far, and you combine the predictions of each model in a simple way (average, weighted average, logistic regression) has no room for too snug.

Unsupervised Learning

7. **Cluster Algorithms**: Grouping consists of grouping a set of objects so that the cluster objects are more similar than those of other clusters.

Each clustering algorithm is different, and here are a few:

- Centroid-based algorithms
- Connectivity-based algorithms
- Density based algorithms
- Probabilistic
- Reduction of dimensionality
- Neural Networks / Deep Learning

8. **Principal Component Analysis**: It is a statistical procedure that uses an orthogonal transformation to convert a set of observations of potentially correlated variables into a set of linearly uncorrelated variable values called principal components.
Some of the PCA applications include compression, data simplification to facilitate learning, visualization. Note that domain knowledge is very important while choosing to go ahead with PCA or not. It is not

appropriate in cases where the data is noisy, (all PCA components have a fairly high variance).

9. **Decomposition of the singular value**: in the linear algebra, the SVD is a factorization of a real complex matrix. For a given matrix m * n M, there exists a decomposition such that M = UΣV, where U and V are unitary matrices and Σ is a diagonal matrix. PCA is a simple SVD application. In computer vision, the first face recognition algorithms used PCA and SVD to represent faces as a linear combination of "Eigen faces," reduce dimensionality, and then match faces to identities through simple methods; Although modern methods are much more sophisticated, many still rely on similar techniques.

10. **Independent Component Analysis**: The ICA is a statistical technique for revealing hidden factors that underlie sets of random variables, measurements, or signals. The ICA defines a generator model for the observed multivariate data, which is usually given as a large sample database. In the model, it is assumed that the data variables are linear mixtures of some unknown latent variables, and the mixing system is also unknown. The latent variables are assumed non-Gaussian and mutually independent and they are called independent components of the observed data.

Machine learning techniques for predictive maintenance

Gaining attention largely due to the rise of the Internet of Things (IoT) and Machine Learning Solutions, Predictive Maintenance brings new data and analytic capabilities to an age-old problem. How do we optimize the productivity of an asset? By enriching operational data with additional contexts such as environmental information and workload data and then applying analytic models, we can predict the risk of failure of assets at a point in time and do so in an automated manner that scales to millions of devices. This allows reducing outages, maintenance costs, and impacts to customers, all contributing to a better quality of service.

1. Application Scenarios

Predictive Maintenance is a defect inspection strategy that uses indicators to prepare for future problems, and as such it's response to the need to be ever more precise in maintenance management by applying data, context, and analytics (machine learning) to the problem space. There are many scenarios where Predictive Maintenance can be crucial, such as:

In Manufacturing, it is highly used to predict vehicle component outages and notify drivers and service technicians or to predict outages in the assembly line process;

In Utilities, it is commonly used to predict outages in power generation equipment, with huge impact on quality of service and maintenance costs;

In Oil and Gas industry, it has been used to develop custom and optimal maintenance schedules for expensive assets such as submersible oil pumps;

In Public Sector, it can be used to balance maintenance services based on citizen usage patterns of services, among many others.

From a business perspective, Predictive Maintenance plays a key role for different business decision-makers: for a COO, that owns the core operational metrics and is ultimately responsible for operational continuity, for a CFO, who will be attracted by the prospect of a reduction in costly unplanned outages, but also by the promise of OpEx savings, or even for a CMO, that cares about customer satisfaction and retaining revenue, as well as trust and reputation.

As an example, in this recent case, by using Microsoft Azure machine learning service, ThyssenKrupp has achieved an unprecedented view into elevator operations and maintenance, now and in the future. The system contains an intelligent information loop: data from elevators is fed into dynamic predictive models, which continually update datasets via seamless integration with Azure. With this, the elevators can teach technicians how to fix them, resulting in dramatically increased elevator uptime.

2. Solution Approach

Maintenance costs are one of the largest factors impacting companies' budget. Attempts to reduce these costs have led to the development of several maintenance strategies and solutions along time. The three basic maintenance policies include:

Corrective Maintenance implies the equipment is repaired after a failure has occurred. As long as the equipment is under a warranty agreement, the equipment owner does not usually pay for the repair though he can experience an unexpected malfunction.

Most equipment is also subject to a Preventive Maintenance policy, which requires performing periodic inspections and other operations at a schedule predetermined by the manufacturer, mostly by time in service. However, this policy does not take into account the actual condition of the equipment as it's scheduled at a fixed time interval.

In contrast, Predictive Maintenance can schedule an intervention based on some sensory information representing the current condition of the equipment and its subsystems and a probability of failure. This approach should, on the one hand, minimize the risk of unexpected failures, which may occur before the next periodic maintenance operation, and on the other hand, reduce the amount of unnecessary preventive maintenance activities.

Predictive Maintenance Challenges

As time maintenance is not enough, the context of use is required, which is where the analytics come in, aiming to "predict" risk of failure for devices with heavy use. It starts with a statistical model that gets better and better (trained) the more information you provide it. This requires the capability to understand the reliability of equipment's at any point in time, to identify and isolate potential failures before they occur; to predict and plan for scheduled maintenance and downtime and to reduce unnecessary time-based maintenance operations. To do this, organizations need to have four things:

1. **Rich Device Data**: To predict and influence equipment's risk of failure, there must be sufficient data on historical behavior to support the prediction. The definition of "sufficient" will vary by industry and context, but in general, the more transactions you can see, and the richer the information associated with those transactions is, the better your ability to predict will be. That data then needs to be coordinated with

metadata (info about channels, prices, locations, etc.) to create a single equipment view.

2. **Flexible Analysis Environment**: An analytics solution can be built incrementally as business needs warrant and allow an increasing range of analytical capabilities to be brought to bear to support maintenance efforts. One key service that will be immediately valuable is Azure Machine Learning, which can be applied against the single equipment view to score the risk of failure at a point in time. These scores can be combined with other equipment context to develop notifications and recommended actions for operations and service staff to take action on.

3. **Ability to Take Action**: Existing production work flow such as dashboards, command centers, and technician portals need to be instrumented to receive notifications and to record the actions taken (or not) based on those notifications.

4. **Operations Feedback Loop**: Once models and recommended actions are created in the analytics environment, their effectiveness needs to be tested. As equipment data connections are already enabled, additional connections to the data representing the action taken need to be developed. Then the actual outages can be compared to others to calculate the accuracy and efficacy of the model, notifications, and resulting actions. The results of all tests can be fed back into the analysis environment to allow optimization of the models.

Machine Learning Implementation

Microsoft also provides a template that helps data scientists easily build and deploy predictive maintenance solutions, which can be found on this public ML Models Gallery.

This predictive maintenance template focuses on the techniques used to predict when an in-service machine will fail so that maintenance can be planned. The template includes a collection of pre-configured machine learning modules, as well as custom R scripts, to enable an end-to-end solution from data processing to deploying of the machine learning model.

Three modeling solutions are provided in this template to accomplish the following tasks:

Regression: Predict the Remaining Useful Life (RUL), or Time to Failure (TTF).

Binary classification: Predict if an asset will fail within the certain time frame (e.g. days).

Multi-class classification: Predict if an asset will fail in different time windows: E.g., fails in window [1, w0] days; fails in the window [w0+1, w1] days; not fail within w1 days

The time units mentioned above can be replaced by working hours, cycles, mileage, transactions, etc., based on the actual scenario.

This template uses the example of simulated aircraft engine run-to-failure events to demonstrate the predictive maintenance modeling process. The implicit assumption of modeling data as done below is that the asset of interest has a progressing degradation pattern, which is reflected in the asset's sensor measurements. By examining the asset's sensor values over time, the machine learning algorithm can learn the relationship between the sensor values and changes in sensor values to the historical failures to predict failures in the future

Machine learning market growth and trends

Many market research reports indicate that the global market for machine learning chips is expected to reach a market size of $ 7.9 billion by 2022, an increase of 9% over the forecast period to A CAGR. A major factor in the popularity of deep learning in the past is that we finally reached a point where we experimented with insightful real world data sets and also abundant computational resources to train precisely huge and robust varieties on these types of data sets. The needs of the most recent programs, for example, training, as well as the assumption of deep varieties of neural networks, often requires exciting advances in computer systems at different stages of the stack. Similarly, the design of fresh and solid hardware units is an incredible incentive and facilitator for analyzing computer devices. A particular primary factor approach to speed up machine learning is to have a quick response time on scientific machine learning tests.

The applications of in-depth learning software that drive the current artificial intelligence revolution have largely functioned on relatively basic computer hardware. Some modern technology giants, such as Google and Intel, have focused their significant resources on the deployment of more specialized computer chips for in-depth learning.

The highly efficient characteristics of advanced learning depend on algorithms called convolutional neural networks, which consist of node layers (also called neurons). These types of neural networks could filter out substantial amounts of information through their "deep" layers to emerge as more advantageous, for example, automatically determining the unique human appearance or understanding different languages. It is usually the varieties of capabilities that previously provide the online services offered by large companies.

Machine learning is already widely used for initiatives comparable to compliance, risk management, and fraudulent activity avoidance. Machine learning is also a good way to automate financial decisions, whether it is solvency assessment or eligibility for an insurance policy.

Machine learning excels at spotting extraordinary variations in transactions, which could mean fraud. Companies ranging from start-ups to behemoths offer these types of solutions.

Although this is merely a short description, machine learning indicates that you can use statistical models and probabilistic algorithms to answer questions; you can easily make educational decisions influenced by our data.

<u>INDEX</u>

www.ingramcontent.com/pod-product-compliance
Lightning Source LLC
Chambersburg PA
CBHW070854070326
40690CB00009B/1842